THE
CHURCH
Saved, United, Empowered

Geoff Ashley

LifeWay Press®
Nashville, Tennessee

Item: 005695956
ISBN: 978-1-4300-3678-4
Dewey decimal classification number: 262
Subject heading: CHURCH \ CHRISTIAN LIFE \ DISCIPLESHIP

Eric Geiger
Vice President, Church Resources

Ed Stetzer
General Editor

Trevin Wax
Managing Editor

Faith Whatley
Director, Adult Ministry

Philip Nation
Director, Adult Ministry Publishing

Joel Polk
Content Editor

We believe that the Bible has God for its author; salvation for its end; and truth, without any mixture of error, for its matter and that all Scripture is totally true and trustworthy. To review LifeWay's doctrinal guideline, please visit *www.lifeway.com/doctrinalguideline*.

Unless otherwise noted, all Scripture quotations are taken from the Holman Christian Standard Bible®, copyright 1999, 2000, 2002, 2003, 2009 by Holman Bible Publishers. Used by permission.

For ordering or inquiries, visit *www.lifeway.com;* write LifeWay Small Groups; One LifeWay Plaza; Nashville, TN 37234-0152; or call toll free (800) 458-2772.

Printed in the United States of America.

Adult Ministry Publishing
LifeWay Church Resources
One LifeWay Plaza
Nashville, Tennessee 37234-0152

TABLE OF CONTENTS

ABOUT THE GOSPEL PROJECT

Some people see the Bible as a collection of stories with morals for life application. But it's so much more. Sure, the Bible has some stories in it, but it's also full of poetry, history, codes of law and civilization, songs, prophecy, letters—even a love letter. When you tie it all together, something remarkable happens. A story is revealed. One story. The story of redemption through Jesus. This is *The Gospel Project*.

When we begin to see the Bible as the story of redemption through Jesus Christ, God's plan to rescue the world from sin and death, our perspective changes. We no longer look primarily for what the Bible says about us but instead see what it tells us about God and what He has done. After all, it's the gospel that saves us, and when we encounter Jesus in the pages of Scripture, the gospel works on us, transforming us into His image. *We become God's gospel project.*

ABOUT THE WRITERS

 Geoff Ashley is the Groups Pastor for The Village Church in Flower Mound, Texas. He received a ThM from Dallas Theological Seminary in 2009 and has been on staff at The Village since 2006, overseeing development of theological resources. He is married to Kaci.

Barry Cram adapted this material for use with small groups.

HOW TO USE THIS STUDY

Welcome to *The Gospel Project*, a gospel-centered small-group study that dives deep into the things of God, lifts up Jesus, focuses on the grand story of Scripture, and drives participants to be on mission. This small-group Bible study provides opportunities to study the Bible and to encounter the living Christ. *The Gospel Project* provides you with tools and resources to purposefully study God's Word and to grow in the faith and knowledge of God's Son. And what's more, you can do so in the company of others, encouraging and building up one another. Here are some things to remember that will help you maximize the usefulness of this resource:

GATHER A GROUP. We grow in the faith best in community with other believers, as we love, encourage, correct, and challenge one another. The life of a disciple of Christ was never meant to be lived alone, in isolation.

PRAY. Pray regularly for your group members.

PREPARE. This resource includes the Bible study content, three devotionals, and discussion questions for each session. Work through the session and devotionals in preparation for each group session. Take notes and record your own questions. Also consider the follow-up questions so you are ready to participate in and add to the discussion, bringing up your own notes and questions where appropriate.

RESOURCE YOURSELF. Make good use of the additional resources available on the Web at *www.gospelproject.com/additionalresources* and search for this specific title. Download a podcast. Read a blog post. Be intentional about learning from others in the faith. For tips on how to better lead groups or additional ideas for leading this Bible study, visit: *www.ministrygrid.com/web/thegospelproject*.

GROUP TIME. Gather together with your group to discuss the session and devotional content. Work through the follow-up questions and your own questions. Discuss the material and the implications for the lives of believers and the mission to which we have been called.

OVERFLOW. Remember, *The Gospel Project* is not just a Bible study. *We* are the project. The gospel is working on us. Don't let your preparation time be simply about the content. Let the truths of God's Word soak in as you study. Let God work on your heart first, and then pray that He will change the hearts of the other people in your group.

THE GOSPEL PROJECT

Session 1

United with a Purpose

That which we would do for Christ if he were here among us we should do for [each] other who are members of the body of Christ.

PETER WALPOT

INDIVIDUAL STUDY

The Word of God is filled with vivid words that depict and describe the people of God—the temple in which God's Spirit dwells, the vine planted and nourished for the glory of God, the flock that Christ shepherds, the bride of Christ, the family of God, etc. Each image provides insight into our individual and corporate identity as the ransomed, rescued, and redeemed.

Perhaps the most dominant image of the church is the body of Christ. As the body of Christ, we are unified in our common salvation and mission. Though our relationship with God is personal, it's never private or completely separated from the rest of God's people.

Why is this "body" language helpful to our understanding of the church?

What other implications are there from understanding the church this way?

Any guy who grew up with an older brother knows what it's like to hear the phrase "Stop hitting yourself." Your brother pins you down, typically by sitting on your chest, overpowers you, and uses your own hand to slap your face. It usually isn't physically painful, but the ego takes a bit of a beating. The "game" may be cruel, but the idea itself is humorous. After all, you don't normally attack yourself. A body tries to protect its various parts rather than do itself harm.

When the apostle Paul used the metaphor of "the body" to describe the church, he focused on our unity—our need to work together for a common cause. If we really are members of the same body, then there should be an underlying love, protection, sympathy, and compassion for each other. Otherwise, we're just some kid lying on the ground hitting ourselves, but this time with no big brother.

In this session, we will consider who we are in light of the biblical depiction of the people of God as the body of Christ. As we do so, we'll see that the body of Christ is joined together and united in one Spirit, in a common experience of suffering and rejoicing, and in a shared opportunity and responsibility to serve each other.

Throughout the week engage these daily study sections on your own. Each of these examines the different ways we are united in Christ as His church. There are three daily readings to prepare you before your group meets for this session. Interact with the Scriptures, and be ready to interact with your small group.

United in the Spirit

¹² For as the body is one and has many parts, and all the parts of that body, though many, are one body—so also is Christ. ¹³ For we were all baptized by one Spirit into one body—whether Jews or Greeks, whether slaves or free—and we were all made to drink of one Spirit. ¹⁴ So the body is not one part but many. ¹⁵ If the foot should say, "Because I'm not a hand, I don't belong to the body," in spite of this it still belongs to the body. ¹⁶ And if the ear should say, "Because I'm not an eye, I don't belong to the body," in spite of this it still belongs to the body. ¹⁷ If the whole body were an eye, where would the hearing be? If the whole body were an ear, where would the sense of smell be? ¹⁸ But now God has placed each one of the parts in one body just as He wanted. ¹⁹ And if they were all the same part, where would the body be? ²⁰ Now there are many parts, yet one body.

1 CORINTHIANS 12:12-20

If you ever find yourself in Europe and you have some money to spend, go shopping for an authentic Black Forest cuckoo clock. You will be in awe of the craftsmanship, both in function and form. Without the benefit of battery or electricity, it keeps accurate time through an intricate and delicate process. Its pendulum, weights, and gears all work together to accomplish a shared goal of timekeeping.

But for all of its sophisticated complexity, a clock is nowhere near as intricate as a living body. Imagine the degree of care and concern that must go into the creation of a person! This truth also speaks to our identity as the body of Christ. If a clockmaker invests so much time in creating this complex mechanism, how much more should we be amazed at the creation of the living organism that is the body of Christ!

> Think about all of the necessary movements that take place for a clock to operate. What would happen if one of the weights were missing or just one of the gears were broken?

> How might this perspective help us understand the importance of individual members contributing to the mission Christ has given us as a body?

As the individual parts of the body are called "members," so the individual persons of the church are called members. Membership is an interesting thing. Many, if not most of us, have been members before in various organizations and entities. We were once members of a high school sports team or the band, boy scouts or girl scouts, honor society or key club, FCA, PTA, or YMCA.

Those who are called the body of Christ share the same breath—the Holy Spirit—who enables and empowers His people for the mission of God. His personal presence is like the blood that pulses through the body and supplies oxygen to live and move. If the Spirit has united us through one faith into one body, then we can assume it is for one purpose. His intentions and plans do not drift aimlessly but are eternal and steadfast.

While the Bible provides various insights into God's intention for His people, one of the most accessible is that we were created to adorn the person and work of Jesus Christ. As people formed by the gospel, we are united to show forth the beauties of the gospel in the way that we love each other (John 17:20-23). Accordingly, the Spirit has composed the body of Christ in order to facilitate our working together to accomplish the mission of the kingdom of God. The more we understand and appreciate the glory of the body of Christ, the more we will be enthralled with the opportunity to contribute to its common good.

What are some potential areas of division in a local church body?

How does staying sensitive to the Spirit help to guard us against unnecessary division?

What are some ways you and your group can practically pursue more faithful and diligent participation in the body?

2 United in Suffering and Rejoicing

²¹ So the eye cannot say to the hand, "I don't need you!" Or again, the head can't say to the feet, "I don't need you!" ²² But even more, those parts of the body that seem to be weaker are necessary. ²³ And those parts of the body that we think to be less honorable, we clothe these with greater honor, and our unpresentable parts have a better presentation. ²⁴ But our presentable parts have no need of clothing. Instead, God has put the body together, giving greater honor to the less honorable, ²⁵ so that there would be no division in the body, but that the members would have the same concern for each other. ²⁶ So if one member suffers, all the members suffer with it; if one member is honored, all the members rejoice with it.

1 CORINTHIANS 12:21-26

Some of the best movies involve loners. There's something in the Western psyche that loves the story of one man against the world. Whether it's Clint Eastwood riding away into a sunset, Bruce Willis taking down terrorists, Tom Hanks beating the elements on an isolated island, or Will Smith surviving a zombie apocalypse, we are enthralled by the image of a lone ranger.

As interesting and entertaining as such stories might be, they often miss the truth that we were created for community. Only in life together can we experience the fullness and joy for which we were created. In fact, of everything that existed in the garden, only one thing was not good—solitude. God said to Adam, "It is not good for man to be alone." Isolation and rugged individualism may be Western ideals, but from a biblical perspective, they are deficient.

As God Himself is a holy community of three distinct Persons, so we were created to dwell in sacred unity in the church. For this reason, we need to embrace the biblical truth that a member cannot survive without a body. Cut off an ear and see how well it survives, much less hears. Though the body might survive the loss of a hand or foot, its function will be hindered greatly—and the appendage itself will not last long once it is amputated!

Which parts of your body would you consider expendable?

What functions would be hindered if these parts were absent?

This is true of the body of Christ as well. Take a member of the church and disconnect him or her from the body. It will not be long before disease and decay begin to happen. Isolation is an enemy in our pursuit of sanctification. Those who honestly think that they don't need the body of Christ are greatly deceived and in great danger: "One who isolates himself pursues selfish desires; he rebels against all sound judgment" (Prov. 18:1). We need each other to survive and thrive as God intended.

Paul wrote that the entire body suffers when any individual member suffers, and the whole body rejoices when a member rejoices. In doing so, he pointed to the interconnected togetherness that marks the body of Jesus Christ.

It is amazing how an injury to one part of the body will cause pain to another. A misaligned back can cause shoulder or leg pain. Compensating for a blister on one foot can cause difficulty in the other. Pretty soon, walking itself becomes a struggle. The same interconnectedness is required for healing as well. A laceration will not heal without coagulants in the blood. And an infection will not clear up without white blood cells. When the body is functioning properly, it experiences both the pain of injury and the joy of healing.

If we are members of the same body, then surely we shall suffer together. There is no way around it unless we isolate ourselves. But isolation only leads to more pain. There is a profound interconnectedness in the body of Christ such that both pain and pleasure extend beyond individual members. It is to be experienced by the entire community of believers. When one member suffers, all suffer. When one is honored, all rejoice.

> What does this notion teach us about individual rights and privileges? In what ways does the gospel affect our perspective of "the individual"?

> What does suffering and rejoicing as the body of Christ communicate to those outside the church?

3 United in Service

²⁷ Now you are the body of Christ, and individual members of it.
²⁸ And God has placed these in the church: first apostles, second prophets, third teachers, next miracles, then gifts of healing, helping, managing, various kinds of languages. ²⁹ Are all apostles? Are all prophets? Are all teachers? Do all do miracles? ³⁰ Do all have gifts of healing? Do all speak in other languages? Do all interpret?
1 CORINTHIANS 12:27-30

The original 1992 Dream Team of Olympic basketball was probably the greatest basketball team of all time. Larry Bird, Magic Johnson, Michael Jordan, Karl Malone, and Charles Barkley not only wowed the world with their art but absolutely dominated the competition. The average game was won by 44 points. In fact, the closest game was decided by 32 points!

The individual talent on the Dream Team was astounding. But what was even more impressive was the way they were able to come together as a solitary unit. Good teams are composed of individuals with complementary skills. What if the 1992 USA team had been composed of five traditional centers or five power forwards? Who would have taken the ball up the court? Or who would have protected the lane and contested shots with a team of point guards?

Think of the body of Christ in a similar way. The church is constituted by various persons having differing gifts, skills, and abilities. This is so much more than a basketball team. The church is the means by which God accomplishes His eternal purposes. Every believer is invited to contribute. Every Christ-follower is invited to participate. The Spirit has so composed the church that it is intended to function as a cohesive unit.

> How can you better steward the various gifts and talents you have been given for the sake of your local congregation?

What structures, organizations, attitudes, or Ideas have you encountered that hinder individuals from using their gifts to serve the body of Christ?

The concept of complementary gifts distributed by the Spirit for the common good of the body and the glory of Christ saturates the biblical text. Consider a few of the places where Paul expounded upon this reality (Rom. 12:4-8; Eph. 4:4-7; 4:15-16), or examine Peter's words in his first letter: "Based on the gift each one has received, use it to serve others, as good managers of the varied grace of God" (1 Pet. 4:10).

Service is an essential implication of the gospel. After all, Christ Himself spoke of His mission as summarized by the idea of service: "For even the Son of Man did not come to be served, but to serve, and to give His life—a ransom for many" (Mark 10:45).

As those who are being conformed to His image, we have a responsibility to mirror and imitate Christ in our serving and preferring others. We have a responsibility to humble ourselves, seek the good of others, and lay down our lives to adorn the glorious gospel of Jesus Christ. This is true in our parenting, marriages, workplaces, social circles, and especially in our churches.

What are some practical ways you might live the life of a servant in your family, among your friends, and in your community?

GROUP STUDY

Warm Up

First Corinthians 12–14 provides the most comprehensive discussion on spiritual gifts in the Bible. For three chapters, Paul wrote about the person of the Holy Spirit and the gifts that He has distributed for the edification and encouragement of the body. Paul wrote that the gifts vary (12:4-5) but that it is the same Spirit who empowers them (12:6) and has distributed them according to His will (12:11).

But right in the middle of all of this is love—the central and preeminent ideal that trumps all gifts and individual activity. We often read the following passage with the married couple in mind. But let's not forget that this passage of Scripture was first given for the sake of the body, the Church of Jesus Christ.

[1] If I speak in the tongues of men or of angels, but do not have love, I am only a resounding gong or a clanging cymbal. [2] If I have the gift of prophecy and can fathom all mysteries and all knowledge, and if I have a faith that can move mountains, but do not have love, I am nothing. [3] If I give all I possess to the poor and give over my body to hardship that I may boast, but do not have love, I gain nothing. [4] Love is patient, love is kind. It does not envy, it does not boast, it is not proud. [5] It does not dishonor others, it is not self-seeking, it is not easily angered, it keeps no record of wrongs. [6] Love does not delight in evil but rejoices with the truth. [7] It always protects, always trusts, always hopes, always perseveres. [8] Love never fails.
1 CORINTHIANS 13:1-8

How have you attempted to love like this within the body of Christ?

Where have you seen this kind of love on display in your church?

Mark Dever says of the body of Christ, "This is no polite and formal fellowship. It's a body, bound together by our individual decisions but also bound together by far more than human decision—the person and work of Christ."[2] If God brings the body together, it will take God's power to keep it together. It's not enough to keep learning new applications of this spiritual truth. We will need to keep learning a new day of surrender so God can continue to work through His people—His Body, His Church.

Discussion

As the body of Christ, the church is the extension of his ministry.[3]
MILLARD J. ERICKSON

We all need each other because we are an extension of Jesus Christ. When we come together, we have the opportunity to express our love to the community. God designed it this way. We are important—each one of us! A voice from church history once said, "Even if the body had only its most important member, it would still be useless without the others."[4] That's another way of saying, "We are only as important as those with whom we serve."

During this time you will have an opportunity to discuss what God revealed to you during the week. See this as a time to serve and minister one to another. Listed below are some of the questions from your daily reading assignments. They will guide your small-group discussion.

1. What are some potential areas of division in a local church body? How does staying sensitive to the Spirit help to guard us against unnecessary division?

2. What are some ways you and your group can practically pursue more faithful and diligent participation in the body?

3. What does this notion teach us about individual rights and privileges? In what ways does the gospel affect our perspective of "the individual"?

4. What does suffering and rejoicing as the body of Christ communicate to those outside the church?

5. How can you better steward the various gifts and talents you have been given for the sake of your local congregation?

6. What structures, organizations, attitudes, or ideas have you encountered that hinder individuals from using their gifts to serve the body of Christ?

7. What are some practical ways you might live the life of a servant in your family, among your friends, and in your community?

Conclusion

Often admonitions to pursue unity are really just subtle admonishments to uniformity. The history of Christian missions is littered with stories of missionaries, many well-intentioned, who equated cultural conformity with conversion. But the clear biblical charge to pursue unity is not a call toward uniformity. God doesn't desire a homogeneous church of clones but a gloriously diverse body that highlights the creativity of God Himself.

As the triune God is three distinct and diverse Persons dwelling in perfect unity, so the church is intended to be composed of varied and assorted members pursuing a similar unity. What a beautiful picture of the gospel to begin to pursue even now—a picture that will one day be fully realized in the age to come with a multitude from every nation, tribe, and tongue as the kings of the earth all bring their own unique glory into the city to come (Rev. 7:9; 21:24).

Spend some time praying this for yourself and for your group:

"God, teach us what Your church looks like as we gather around Your resurrected Son. Lead us to suffer with those who suffer and rejoice with those who rejoice. Help us to serve one another in love and humility. Give us the ability to obey You as we express Jesus Christ in our neighborhoods and communities. Amen."

1. Peter Walpot, "The True Yieldedness and the Christian Community of Goods," in *Early Anabaptist Spirituality,* ed. Daniel Liechty (Mahwah, NJ: Paulist Press, 1994), 179.
2. Mark Dever, *What is a Healthy Church?* (Wheaton: Crossway, 2007), 26.
3. Theodoret of Cyr, *Commentary on the First Epistle to the Corinthians 247,* quoted in *1–2 Corinthians,* ed. Gerald Bray, vol. VII in *Ancient Christian Commentary: New Testament* (Downers Grove: IVP, 1999), 123.
4. Millard J. Erickson, *Christian Theology,* 3rd ed. (Grand Rapids: Baker, 2013), 961.
5. Augustine, *Letters 99,* quoted in *1–2 Corinthians,* ed. Gerald Bray, vol. VII in *Ancient Christian Commentary: New Testament* (Downers Grove: IVP, 1999), 128.

Far be it from us to refuse to hear what is bitter and sad
to those whom we love. It is not possible for one member
to suffer without the other members suffering with it. [5]

AUGUSTINE

NOTES

Session 2

A House for God

The church is the temple of the living God ... built on the foundations of the prophets and apostles, with Jesus Christ as the chief cornerstone. [1]

MICHAEL BIRD

INDIVIDUAL STUDY

The world is filled with glorious temples. The ancient complex of Angkor Wat in northern Cambodia, the largest religious monument in the world, is overwhelming. Standing in the shadow of the "Great Buddha" in Japan would make one feel small and insignificant, even if only for a moment. Most temples or shrines are breathtaking and beautiful. But that's the nature of temples—to be grand and glorious, to bring all eyes and attention upon the one for whom it was built. They hold significant places of honor and meaning within their respective religions.

What comes to mind when you hear the word *temple*? What do think temples represent? *Worship — Religion / holy place.*

The disciples experienced awe and wonder in Jerusalem. Staring at the beauty of King Herod's temple, these men were amazed at the profound size and scope of the temple complex (Matt. 24:1-2). Even the solitary stones that encircled the grounds were incredible (Mark 13:1-2). Seeking to win influence with the Jews, Herod had spared no expense in decorating the center of Jewish life and worship.

Therefore, it must have been all the more surprising to hear from Jesus that this temple would soon fall and fade away from the center of Jewish life. Jesus once said, "Destroy this temple, and I will raise it again in three days" (see John 2:19 NIV). Even today that would be quite a feat, but imagine such a construction project without electricity or engines! Of course, Christ wasn't talking about Herod's temple anymore. He was speaking of His own body. Herod's temple was eventually burned and torn down, but Christ's body has long since been buried and raised. As the Son of God said, "Something greater than the temple is here!" (Matt. 12:6). Jesus Christ Himself is the temple of God. He is the union of divinity and humanity; He is where God and man meet. No longer was man to meet God in a place but rather in a Person.

In this session, we'll consider who we are from the perspective of a temple of God—the people in whom God resides. In the Old Testament, the temple referred to a place. In the New Testament, the temple refers to a people. Christ is the foundation of this sanctuary where the Spirit lives. As Christians, we're being built together as God's residence—a beacon of hope to the world.

Throughout the week engage these daily study sections on your own. Each of these examines the different aspects of what it means to be the house of God. There are three daily readings to prepare you before your group meets for this session. Interact with the Scriptures, and be ready to interact with your small group.

Foundation of the Church

The apostle Paul spoke of the church in various ways: the body of Christ, God's field, God's building. In his First Letter to the Corinthians, Paul continued with the building analogy by speaking of Christ as the foundation:

> ⁹ For we are God's coworkers. You are God's field, God's building. ¹⁰ According to God's grace that was given to me, I have laid a foundation as a skilled master builder, and another builds on it. But each one must be careful how he builds on it. ¹¹ For no one can lay any other foundation than what has been laid down. That foundation is Jesus Christ. ¹² If anyone builds on that foundation with gold, silver, costly stones, wood, hay, or straw, ¹³ each one's work will become obvious, for the day will disclose it, because it will be revealed by fire; the fire will test the quality of each one's work. ¹⁴ If anyone's work that he has built survives, he will receive a reward. ¹⁵ If anyone's work is burned up, it will be lost, but he will be saved; yet it will be like an escape through fire. ¹⁶ Don't you yourselves know that you are God's sanctuary and that the Spirit of God lives in you? ¹⁷ If anyone destroys God's sanctuary, God will destroy him; for God's sanctuary is holy, and that is what you are.
>
> 1 CORINTHIANS 3:9-17

One of my favorite urban legends is about a college campus where the library is slowly sinking. The architect planned for the wood and concrete, for the desks and chairs and windows, but not for the weight of the thousands upon thousands of books the library would house. As a result, his foundation was insufficient and the library slowly began descending into the soil.

This story reminds us of the importance of a foundation. Without a sufficient foundation, whatever is built on top will surely suffer. As the saying goes, "You are only as strong as your foundation."

Have you ever experienced the disruption of a faulty foundation—at home, at work, in the city? What was the result?

What implications do you think this image will have as we think about Christ as our foundation?

The church in Corinth was a mess. People were picking their favorite apostles. A man was sleeping with his dad's wife. Members were suing each other in public courts. Rich people were hording food and getting drunk at the Lord's Table. The church was divided, and Paul wasn't amused! But the apostle never gave up on the church. Too much was at stake. Paul had spent more than a year there laboring for the sake of the gospel (Acts 18:11). He had revisited them and written various letters. In these things, he went back to the basics and started again with the foundational truths of the gospel.

When Paul wrote about the church as a temple of God, he did what any good builder does—he laid a foundation. The foundation is the first and most important part of any building project. If the church is to survive, it must have a strong, solid, and sustaining foundation. Thankfully, we have just such a foundation in Christ Jesus.

There are many things we can build our lives on: our profession, family, money, leisure, or other passions and purposes. But only one foundation will truly stand. No matter who you are or what you do, you cannot lay a faultless foundation apart from faith in the life, death, and resurrection of Jesus Christ. As Paul wrote, "No one can lay any other foundation than that which has been laid down" (1 Cor. 3:11).

The life, death, and resurrection of Jesus Christ—the center of the good news of God's kingdom—stands as the only foundation that will withstand the shifts and storms of life. If our lives are to be built upon the foundation of Jesus Christ, then the same should be true of our churches. After all, the church itself is the pillar and foundation of the truth (1 Tim. 3:15).

Describe the symptoms of a "faulty foundation" in your personal life. What are the things that tempt you to build upon these foundations?

What about our churches? What are some common "faulty foundations" we tend to pursue? Why are these foundations so appealing?

2 Temple of the Holy Spirit

We've seen how the people of God are God's building and Christ is the cornerstone, but what kind of building are we? What is inside this holy place? Paul spoke to this question too. Watch how he described a Christian as a temple, a sanctuary of the Holy Spirit:

> [19] Don't you know that your body is a sanctuary of the Holy Spirit who is in you, whom you have from God? You are not your own, [20] for you were bought at a price. Therefore glorify God in your body.
>
> 1 CORINTHIANS 6:19-20

Both the tabernacle in the wilderness and the temple of Jerusalem included a particular place in which God's glory rested in a unique and distinct manner. Above the Ark of the Covenant, God's presence was manifested. This was the heart of both the tabernacle and the temple.

Can you imagine the elaborate process of building the temple? Consider the time and detail that must have gone into the work and the difficult reality of moving timber and stone to the heights of Jerusalem from the Mediterranean coast. This was no weekend building project; it was a tedious task marked by the dedication and sacrifice of an entire nation. First built by Solomon at the apex of Israel's Old Testament history, the temple must have been profoundly beautiful. By itself, it was certainly majestic. It was to be the dwelling place of Living God— not the "so-called gods" of the surrounding pagan nations, but the God of all creation! The God who created and sustains all things manifested His presence in a unique way within the complex at the center of Israel's faith and practice as a testimony to the nations.

What ideas and beliefs are communicated by a temple to those on the outside? What would it take for you to be drawn to visiting a temple?

When the Scriptures speak of the church as the sanctuary or temple of the Holy Spirit, it communicates a very distinct and meaningful idea that the omnipresent God dwells within His particular people. There are numerous implications of this precious and powerful gospel truth, but perhaps the most immediate is that there is an inherent call upon our lives toward holiness. God's sanctuary is holy, and that is what you are (1 Cor. 3:17).

The English word "sanctuary" shares the same root as "sanctification," the process of being made holy. A sanctuary is a holy place, a place (or people, in this context) that has been "set apart" for the worship of God (1 Pet. 2:1-5). The church is "a holy priesthood" (2:9). As such, we are called into the glorious work of proclaiming the praises of our Great High Priest, Jesus Christ (Heb. 2:17; 3:1; 4:14-15). As the external beauty of Solomon's temple communicated the majesty of God, so now the internal beauty of the church communicates His glorious grace.

With the Levitical Law in mind, Peter said to pursue holiness for a simple reason—God is holy:

> 13 Therefore, with minds that are alert and fully sober, set your hope
> on the grace to be brought to you when Jesus Christ is revealed at his
> coming. 14 As obedient children, do not conform to the evil desires you
> had when you lived in ignorance. 15 But just as he who called you is holy,
> so be holy in all you do; 16 for it is written: "Be holy, because I am holy."
> 1 PETER 1:13-16

Unfortunately, holiness isn't always a visible mark of many who would call themselves Christians today. If you were to ask one hundred random strangers the first adjective that comes to mind when they think of Christians, how many would say "holy"? If we were honest with one another, we'd probably admit that "holy" isn't the first word that comes to our minds when we think of ourselves either. And yet holiness is fundamental to our identity. Because God is holy and dwells within us, we are to be holy in all of our conduct. We are to be set apart, sacred, different, and distinct from our surrounding culture.

> How do you "practice" or pursue holiness? What does that look like
> Sunday through Saturday?

> What should our identity as God's temple communicate to the nations today?

We saw earlier how Paul spoke of the church as the sanctuary of God. Now we see him saying that the Christian's body is a sanctuary of the Spirit. As a result of the indwelling presence of the Spirit and the redemption accomplished through Christ, we are urged toward sanctification. The Spirit who testifies of Christ will transform the church to the image of Christ. Since God's glory rests in us, it should flow out from us. We glorify God by the pursuit of holiness. Compelled by love, we die to ourselves and live for Christ, seeking sanctification by the Spirit.

3 Being Built Together as God's Residence

We've seen that Jesus is the cornerstone of the church—the temple of God. We've seen that the Spirit of God has taken up residence in us, both individually and corporately. And now we see how God is building us together as His dwelling place. In his Letter to the Ephesians, Paul made this point clear:

> [19] So then you are no longer foreigners and strangers, but fellow citizens with the saints , and members of God's household, [20] built on the foundation of the apostles and prophets, with Christ Jesus Himself as the cornerstone. [21] The whole building, being put together by Him, grows into a holy sanctuary in the Lord. [22] You also are being built together for God's dwelling in the Spirit.
> EPHESIANS 2:19-22

What image comes into your mind when you think of a castle? Perhaps it's Buckingham or Windsor, royal domiciles for the British monarchy. Those familiar with medieval lore might picture moats and drawbridges, walls and towers. People from the East may think of parallel walls, gardens, and shrines.

Castles have played a major part of our entertainment culture. One considers the image of Dracula's castle, dark and gloomy and perched upon an impregnable mountain. Others think of the castles from Sleeping Beauty and Cinderella, creations of Disney patterned after Neuschwanstein in southern Germany. Though originally designed primarily for defensive fortification, castles always had a sense of nobility. They were truly "fit for a king" in form and function.

What adjectives would you use to describe the dwelling place of royalty or some other form of dignitary?

To what degree do you see yourself in the same manner?

In the passage above, Paul used the metaphor of the body of Christ to build an understanding of the church's role as God's royal residence. Having established the foundation of one body comprised of both Jew and Gentile in verses 11-18, the apostle wrote of the church as being a united household—a dwelling place for God (v. 22). Stop and think about the implications of this incredible statement: The church is the residence of God. The Creator of all things lives not just with His people, but within all of His people.

But this temple isn't finished yet! We are "being built together." As individual stones come together to make up a castle's walls, so individual Christians come together to form a dwelling place for our King. This should provide great hope to us who look around and see division and distrust and disorder in the church. God is not yet finished accomplishing His purposes. He is the one building His church together.

Since God is continually building this house for Himself, how might we make ourselves more receptive to this work?

In what ways are we responsible to cooperate with God in His endeavor?

Paul described himself as a skilled master builder. This was no arrogant boast but rather a reference to his apostolic passion, gifting, and authority. Paul's goal, his mission and purpose in life, was to lay a foundation of faith in Jesus Christ. He partnered with God in the hard work of building, and we can, too.

GROUP STUDY

Warm Up

This session focuses primarily on the whole congregation as God's sacred temple. Let's take the next few moments to focus on what it means for each of us personally. Read aloud the Scriptures listed below, and then answer the discussion questions together. All of these verses focus on glorifying God with our bodies as the temple of God. This is possible only because of the indwelling power of the Holy Spirit.

"But put on the Lord Jesus Christ, and make no
plans to satisfy the fleshly desires."
ROMANS 13:14

"Therefore, whether you eat or drink, or whatever
you do, do everything for God's glory."
1 CORINTHIANS 10:31

"For Christ's love compels us, since we have reached this conclusion: If One
died for all, then all died. And He died for all so that those who live should no
longer live for themselves, but for the One who died for them and was raised."
2 CORINTHIANS 5:14-15

"Therefore, dear friends, since we have such promises, let us
cleanse ourselves from every impurity of the flesh and spirit,
completing our sanctification in the fear of God."
2 CORINTHIANS 7:1

Discuss the individual privileges and responsibilities that come with being God's temple.

What compels you to live for something "bigger" and beyond yourself?

Describe how your community of faith helps you pursue holiness on a personal level. How do you contribute to this cause for others?

Discussion

Those in whom the Spirit comes to live are God's new Temple. They are, individually and corporately, places where heaven and earth meet. [2]

N. T. WRIGHT

In the Old Testament, there was an expectation to keep the temple pure and undefiled. God always gave specific instructions concerning what would be appropriate and inappropriate behavior inside His temple. In the New Testament, the expectation and instruction is no less important. The purpose of "God's House" is to bring glory to God and to sanctify his name—in the Old Testament and the New.

During this time you will have an opportunity to discuss what God revealed to you during the week. Listed below are some of the questions from your daily reading assignments. They will guide your small-group discussion.

1. What comes to mind when you hear the word *temple*? What do think temples represent?

2. What implications do you think this image will have as we think about Christ as our foundation?

3. Describe the symptoms of a "faulty foundation" in your personal life. What are the things that tempt you to build upon these foundations?

4. What about our churches? What are some common "faulty foundations" that local churches pursue? Why are these foundations so appealing?

5. How do you "practice" or pursue holiness? What does that look like Sunday through Saturday?

6. What adjectives would you use to describe the dwelling place of royalty or some other form of dignitary? To what degree do you see yourself in the same manner?

7. Since God is continually building this house for Himself, how might we make ourselves more receptive to this work? How are we responsible to cooperate with God in His endeavor?

Conclusion

From the Old Testament to the New, the Lord God is a God who dwells among His people. God has a royal residence, but it is not a sanctuary of humankind's own making (Acts 17:24). It is a dwelling place formed by God Himself—the body of Jesus Christ: "The Word became flesh and took up residence among us. We observed His glory, the glory as the One and Only Son from the Father, full of grace and truth" (John 1:14). In the incarnation, the shadows and flickers of Old Testament light find final fulfillment in Jesus. He is the anticipated and expected realization of hope and desire.

As God's temple, we look forward to the day when the whole earth is filled with the manifested presence of God:

> [22] I did not see a sanctuary in it, because the Lord God the Almighty and the Lamb are its sanctuary. [23] The city does not need the sun or the moon to shine on it, because God's glory illuminates it, and its lamp is the Lamb. [24] The nations will walk in its light, and the kings of the earth will bring their glory into it. [25] Each day its gates will never close because it will never be night there. [26] They will bring the glory and honor of the nations into it.
> REVELATION 21:22-26

Spend some time praying this for yourself and for your group:

> "God, use us for Your glory. We welcome You here forever and always. We rest on the foundation of Jesus Christ, Your Son. Show us what we need to do for You that we might reflect Your goodness and greatness to our community. Amen."

1. Michael Bird, *Evangelical Theology* (Grand Rapids: Zondervan, 2013), 717.
2. N. T. Wright, *Simply Christian* (New York: Harper-Collins, 2006), 129.
3. Chrysostom, *Homilies on the Epistles of Paul to the Corinthians* 8.7, quoted in *1–2 Corinthians*, ed. Gerald Bray, vol. VII in *Ancient Christian Commentary: New Testament* (Downers Grove: IVP, 1999), 32.

Let us not merely cling to Christ, but let us be cemented
to Him, for if we stand apart, we shall perish. [3]
JOHN CHRYSOSTOM

NOTES

THE GOSPEL PROJECT

Session 3

Tomorrow's Reality for Today

The life and fellowship of Christians in history is to be a
foretaste of life in the Kingdom of God and is to reflect in
the world something of what the [future] will be. [1]

GEORGE ELDON LADD

INDIVIDUAL STUDY

For those who grew up watching Saturday morning cartoons, the first glimpse of a futuristic world came our way in a little show called *The Jetsons*. What kid wouldn't be fascinated by flying cars and robot maids? Sometime later, we were able to see a different vision of the future through the eyes of Robert Zemeckis' second installment in the *Back to the Future* series. It just kept getting better—holographic movie previews, hover-board technology, and self-fitting and drying jackets and shoes.

What's interesting and constant about the Hollywood picture of the future is that it isn't perfect. There are the blatantly dystopian visions of the future—*The Terminator, The Hunger Games,* and *The Matrix* to name a few. But even the seemingly happier visions of the future have underlying conflict. After all, a movie without conflict isn't much of a story.

> **How does the picture of a perfect and peaceful future look like to you? Stop and imagine how that would make you feel. What do you look forward to the most?**

A glorious eternity is precisely the picture that emerges from the pages of Scripture. Even more amazing, the Bible presents the church as a foretaste of this faultless and unfading future. We are the presence of the future, a present colony of heaven to be fully populated at the consummation of our marriage to the Bridegroom. And because this future world is soon coming, its beauty penetrates and permeates the present as we look forward to the future.

In this session, we will see what it means for the church to be the presence of the future—a foretaste today of the new world God has promised to establish. As God's future-minded people, we seek what is above, live as a colony of heaven, and actively anticipate the day we will join Christ at the marriage supper of the Lamb as His bride.

Throughout the week engage these daily study sections on your own. Each of these examines the different aspects of God's future promise for the here-and-now. There are three daily readings to prepare you before your group meets for this session. Interact with the Scriptures, and be ready to interact with your small group.

We Set Our Minds on Future Glory

> [1] So if you have been raised with the Messiah, seek what is above, where the Messiah is, seated at the right hand of God. [2] Set your minds on what is above, not on what is on the earth. [3] For you have died, and your life is hidden with the Messiah in God. [4] When the Messiah, who is your life, is revealed, then you also will be revealed with Him in glory.
>
> COLOSSIANS 3:1-4

Humans love to seek, and the Bible teaches that the act of seeking and searching is a good thing (especially if you're seeking what is good). For instance, Jesus said that the kingdom of God is like a treasure hidden in a field. He commanded us to seek first the kingdom and God's righteousness, to ask, seek, and knock (Matt. 6:33; 7:7-8). Nothing is more natural and necessary than searching, seeking, and looking.

In Colossians 3:1-4, Paul pointed to this broad biblical command and specified the direction of our desire. Since Christ is in heaven, we are to look there. He is our treasure and joy! Life and purpose and pleasure are not buried in the ground but raised into the heavens and seated at the right hand of the Father.

Embedded in this passage are two parallel commands. We are to seek and set our minds on what is above. Rather than thinking of them as different, it is important to see how they complement each other. After all, we will naturally seek the desires and obsessions of our hearts and minds.

What in life are you seeking/pursuing the most? What do you spend the majority of your time thinking about?

While pursuing these goals, what seems to get in your way the most—lack of time, talent, external factors, etc.?

What we most treasure, we seek. As many have noted, the greatest gift of the gospel is that we get God Himself. Since He is our treasure, it stands to reason that we would naturally yearn to seek after Him more and more.

This is reflected in the words of the psalmist:

> [1] God, You are my God; I eagerly seek You. I thirst for You; my body faints for You in a land that is dry, desolate, and without water. [2] So I gaze on You in the sanctuary to see Your strength and Your glory. [3] My lips will glorify You because Your faithful love is better than life.
>
> PSALM 63:1-3

We could look at other passages in order to emphasize this point further (see Isa. 26:7-9; Phil. 3:7-11). The Bible says we are to seek what is above as a general pattern for our lives in Christ. Do not confuse this with New-Age spirituality or Buddhist longing for nirvana. Our seeking is not mindless meditation. We are not searching for purpose; rather, we are searching for a Person. Our purpose has already been revealed, and it is fixed upon this Person, Jesus Christ.

Take another look at Col 3:4: "When the Messiah, who is your life, is revealed, then you also will be revealed with Him in glory." We are to think about this future revelation of the Son of God and the effect it will have upon us. This future picture of what Christ will do and this future idea of "who we will be" reaches back into the present. The Christian's "tomorrow" infuses "today" with passion and purpose.

How would you describe your devotion to Jesus? What kind of words do you use when you talk about your relationship with Him?

Are you comfortable using words like treasure, savor, desire, or cherish? Why or why not?

We Are a Colony of Heaven

¹⁷ Join in imitating me, brothers, and observe those who live according to the example you have in us. ¹⁸ For I have often told you, and now say again with tears, that many live as enemies of the cross of Christ. ¹⁹ Their end is destruction; their god is their stomach; their glory is in their shame. They are focused on earthly things, ²⁰ but our citizenship is in heaven, from which we also eagerly wait for a Savior, the Lord Jesus Christ. ²¹ He will transform the body of our humble condition into the likeness of His glorious body, by the power that enables Him to subject everything to Himself.

PHILIPPIANS 3:17-21

James Fenimore Cooper's *The Last of the Mohicans* is set in the American colonies during the 18th-century French and Indian War. In the movie version of the story, there is a scene in which a supporting character, Major Duncan Heyward has a conversation with a superior. In complete disagreement with the officer's direction, he proclaims, "I thought British policy was 'Make the world England.'" That line sums up the idea of "colonialism."

Colonization isn't looked upon favorably today. The concept has been diluted and tarnished by a history of negative examples. So, when we think of the church as a colony of heaven, we might enter the conversation already predisposed toward suspicion. Fortunately, the Bible redeems the images that humankind has corrupted. We can recapture the beauty and glory to be found therein.

> **In Philippians 3:17-21, how does Paul see our heavenly citizenship? What are the implications concerning the way we live on earth?**

Originally a colonial outpost of Rome, Philippi had long enjoyed the privileges of citizenship. From what we know of that time and place, most Philippians would have been quite proud of their citizenship. (Citizenship in the Roman Empire was a precious thing.) So when Paul describes this new society of Jesus-follower as a colony of heaven, he's subverting the Roman authority of the day. If a Christian's citizenship is in God's kingdom, this makes Paul's words pretty incredible. Some might have even considered them treasonous.

For Paul, the truest and most important citizenship of Christians was not to Rome but to the kingdom of God. Thus, as a natural implication, ultimate allegiance would not be owed to Caesar but to Christ. He alone is Lord. For us today, this means that even if our passports are stamped with the seal of the USA, the UK, or the UAE, it is ultimately the Lord to whom we belong.

What should a citizen of heaven be known for? What characteristics should be true of our kingdom identity?

The church is called to bring life and light to the world, to bear fruit and multiply through the work of discipleship. As a colony of heaven, the church is a gathering of citizens of God's kingdom in glad-hearted submission to a generous and good King.

Peter described a Christian's life as one of exile. "Dear friends, I urge you as strangers and temporary residents to abstain from fleshly desires that war against you" (1 Pet. 2:11). A first-century audience saturated by Old Testament hope would instantly recognize the identity of strangers and temporary residents. Other translations speak of sojourners, exiles, aliens, and pilgrims.

Peter again helps us: "Conduct yourselves honorably among the Gentiles, so that in a case where they speak against you as those who do what is evil, they will, by observing your good works, glorify God on the day of visitation" (1 Pet. 2:12).

Our waiting is to be marked not by a casual apathy but by a general sense of goodwill and the active pursuit of good deeds. Looking back at Major Heyward's quote from *The Last of the Mohicans*, we can see that in some sense the goal of colonization from a biblical perspective is exactly what he articulated. If British policy was "Make the world England," then the biblical mandate is "Make the world heaven." Only Jesus will bring heaven to earth, but we as His people are called to be a foretaste of that future.

We are a colony of heaven, and our ultimate hope and expectation is that heaven will come to earth and we will be transformed. For this we wait—not passively like sitting in a doctor's office waiting to be seen. But we wait actively like a server waiting tables at a restaurant.

What's the difference between waiting in a doctor's office and waiting tables? Write down the different attitudes and actions between the two.

What do you enjoy doing the most while waiting for Christ's return?

serving him each & everyday

(Abundant life)

3 We Are the Bride of Christ

As we have considered the images of body and temple, so we now turn to that of bride. Who are we? We are the bride of Christ. And the Bible speaks of a day in which our marriage to Christ will be consummated in unending joy. The last book of the Bible paints a picture of a glorious wedding feast, with Jesus as the groom and the church as the bride:

> [6] Then I heard something like the voice of a vast multitude, like the sound of cascading waters, and like the rumbling of loud thunder, saying: Hallelujah, because our Lord God, the Almighty, has begun to reign! [7] Let us be glad, rejoice, and give Him glory, because the marriage of the Lamb has come, and His wife has prepared herself. [8] She was given fine linen to wear, bright and pure. For the fine linen represents the righteous acts of the saints. [9] Then he said to me, "Write: Those invited to the marriage feast of the Lamb are fortunate!" He also said to me, "These words of God are true."
>
> REVELATION 19:6-9

Since we are the bride of Christ, perhaps no other metaphor better communicates our role as the "presence of the future" than that of wedding engagement. For every couple who have walked down the aisle, they understand that a wedding takes a lot of preparation. The rehearsal, the dress, tuxedos, the reception, and don't forget the dress! All of it takes time, energy, and money. Even the simplest of celebrations will require some time to plan. The day is a special one, and it deserves our most thoughtful consideration.

What was the most elaborate wedding you have ever attended?
What was the most simple?

As the bride of Christ, we are to make ourselves ready for the coming marriage supper, the consummation of our faith and hope. We have something to do as we wait. Until the final glorious day, our duties are not done. As final preparations are being made through the rehearsal and into the day of the wedding, so provision is being made constantly by the saints for that blessed feast. The Bible speaks of at least two separate tasks that the saints are to carry out in preparation for our future—evangelism and good works.

Evangelism. "Those invited to the marriage feast of the Lamb are fortunate!" In Luke 14:12-24, Jesus tells a story known as the parable of the great banquet. In this parable, a powerful man is throwing a party, and he sends out invitations to attend this event of the year. Unfortunately, all who were invited offered various excuses and refused to attend. Thus, the master sends out his servants near and far to invite others into the feast, saying, "Go out into the highways and lanes and make them come in, so that my house may be filled" (v. 23).

We are like the servants compelled to "go out into the highways and lanes and make them come in." We are to "go and make disciples of all nations" (Matt. 28:19). Or, as Paul would write, because of the reconciling work of God, "we are ambassadors for Christ, certain that God is appealing through us. We plead on Christ's behalf, 'Be reconciled to God'" (2 Cor. 5:20).

Good Works. "She was given fine linen to wear, bright and pure. For the fine linen represents the righteous acts of the saints" (Rev. 19:8). In addition to inviting others to join in the feast, the bride has the responsibility to adorn herself with good works.

Good works are an evidence of the internal wonder of faith. As the righteousness of Christ is imputed to us in the gospel, so it flows through us and creates an actual righteousness in us that begins to transform our lives. God looks upon the heart (1 Sam. 16:7), but His seeing doesn't stop there. Why? Because the heart is made evident by the hands and feet that follow wherever the heart leads. Those who love goodness and holiness and justice will pursue those things and thus adorn themselves accordingly. Those who consider others greater than themselves and have minds and hearts set on what is above will gladly serve Christ by serving His body. Those who are the bride of Christ will prepare themselves for this glorious day.

What are some good works that "adorn" the gospel and prepare us for the wedding day?

How is God calling you to partner with Him as He continually invites others to the wedding feast?

GROUP STUDY

Warm Up

Take a moment to read these quotes about the church from the past and present. Answer the questions below to get the discussion started.

What we desire now is not present, but let us not falter in desire; let long, continuous desire be our daily exercise, because the one who made the promise, doesn't cheat us. [2]

AUGUSTINE

If you are a Christian, you are not a citizen of this world trying to get to heaven. You are a citizen of heaven making your way through this world. [3]

VANCE HAVNER

The church there was a colony of heaven. It was a little bit of heaven set down in a pagan world. Its citizens were to permeate its environment with the principles of heaven. [4]

HERSCHEL HOBBS

It is safe to tell the pure in heart that they shall see God, for only the pure in heart want to. [5]

C. S. LEWIS

How do you experience and live the kingdom of heaven here on earth? In what ways does it impact the lost world around you?

If you could change one thing about your community of faith while you wait for God's promised future, what would it be?

Discussion

How fascinating and completely unimaginable it is to conceive of a future in which conflict and struggle are completely eradicated! A world where death, disease, sickness, sorrow, and sin are undone, all that is wrong is made right.

During this time you will have an opportunity to discuss what you have imagined about the future. Listed below are some of the questions from your daily reading assignments. They will guide your small-group discussion.

1. What in life are you seeking/pursuing the most? What do you spend the majority of your time thinking about?

2. While pursuing these goals, what seems to get in your way the most—lack of time, talent, external factors, etc.?

3. How would you describe your devotion to Jesus? What kind of words do you use when you talk about your relationship with Him?

4. Are you comfortable using words like treasure, savor, desire, or cherish? Why or why not?

5. In Philippians 3:17-21, how does Paul see our heavenly citizenship? What are the implications concerning the way we live on earth?

6. Think about the difference between waiting in a doctor's office and waiting tables at a restaurant. Discuss the difference between them.

7. What should a citizen of heaven be known for? What characteristics should be true of our kingdom identity?

Conclusion

The image of the foreigner, stranger, sojourner or alien is a major biblical archetype. Its meaning is fluid, shifting from the literal status of the OT patriarchs and the nation of Israel to the NT emphasis on Christians as people whose citizenship is in heaven rather than on earth... The foreigner lives in a double awareness: a sense of an identity that has been lost or forfeited, and an awareness of being homeless or strange in his or her current environment. [6]

DICTIONARY OF BIBLICAL IMAGERY

As strangers in a foreign land, who are we? We are the bride of Christ. We are a colony of heaven. We are a people with hearts and minds set on future glory. We are the present-day hope for the future of all who will believe.

Spend some time praying this for yourself and for your group:

"God, reveal to us a greater measure of You and Your kingdom. Teach us what it means to be a true colony of heaven in a foreign land. Give us opportunities to share You with the lost world. Amen."

1. George Eldon Ladd, *A Theology of the New Testament* (Grand Rapids: Eerdmans, 1993), 586-87.
2. Augustine, *Sermons* 350A.4, quoted in *Colossians, 1–2 Thessalonians, 1–2 Timothy, Titus, Philemon,* ed. Peter Gorday, vol. IX in *Ancient Christian Commentary: New Testament* (Downers Grove: IVP, 2000), 47.
3. Vance Havner, quoted in *The Westminster Collection of Christian Quotations,* comp. Martin H. Manser (Louisville: Westminster John Knox Press, 2001), 165.
4. Herschel Hobbs, *Baptist Faith and Message* (Nashville: LifeWay, 1971), 68.
5. C. S. Lewis, *The Problem of Pain* (New York: Touchstone, 1996), 130.
6. "Foreigner," in *Dictionary of Biblical Imagery,* gen. eds. Leland Ryken, James C. Wilhoit, and Tremper Longman III (Downers Grove: IVP, 1998), 300.
7. G. K. Beale, *We Become What We Worship* (Downers Grove: IVP, 2008), 22.

We resemble what we revere, either for restoration or ruin. [7]

G. K. BEALE

NOTES

THE
GOSPEL
PROJECT

Session 4

Sent Into
the World

INDIVIDUAL STUDY

"Unite us!" Shout those words to young men who have seen the movie *Braveheart,* and they'll probably hear you speaking in a Scottish accent, whether you used one or not. Our minds race to William Wallace speaking with Robert the Bruce about the need to unite the clans of Scotland in rebellion against the English. Say these words and someone might respond by yelling, "Freedom!"

Who doesn't love stories of people coming together, united in the common pursuit of one goal? Following a charismatic leader, driven by a shared passion, they forge ahead toward the prize.

> What are some examples of people coming together around a common cause?

> How are these examples similar to or different from the unity of the church?

The Bible paints a stunning portrait of the church as holy and passionate—sent into the world in obedience to Jesus Christ. We've seen how the church is comprised of various members, but these members form one body. We are Christ's body, the temple of the Holy Spirit, and the presence of the future.

In this session, we will consider our roles and responsibilities as one holy, apostolic church. As God's people, we are called to be of one heart and mind, set apart from the world, and on mission to further spread the good news of Jesus Christ that we received from the apostles. Our unity, holiness, and passion for the truth aid us in our mission as God's people in the world.

Throughout the week engage these daily study sections on your own. Each of these examines the different aspects of our mission in the world. There are three daily readings to prepare you before your group meets for this session. Interact with the Scriptures, and be ready to interact with your small group.

We Are One in Heart and Mind

> Now the large group of those who believed were of one heart
> and mind, and no one said that any of his possessions was his
> own, but instead they held everything in common.
> ACTS 4:32

"What's mine is yours." It's one thing to say this if you are poor. It's another thing to live by this saying if you are person of means. This distinctive characteristic of generosity set apart the Christian church in the first century.

> Consider how strange the actions of the early believers must have
> been to outsiders. What reasons would you give to explain the early
> church's behavior?

Reading through the beginning of Acts, we find some pretty interesting events. Skipping over tongues of fire, strange speech and all of that, think about how our ancestors in the faith spent their time. The Scriptures specify that they devoted themselves to sharing meals, fellowship, prayer, and the apostolic teaching (Acts 2:42). Most churches have a hard time getting the majority of their members to gather for a weekly or monthly night of prayer, and yet the early church assembled "every day" (Acts 2:46). What gives?

The gospel is what gives! The gospel changed the hearts and minds of these men and women such that their entire priorities were reoriented. Work, family, leisure, and more all became secondary. Spreading the kingdom of God and living as the body of Christ became primary.

In order to understand the church in Acts, it might be helpful to go back to our consideration of the metaphor of the church as the body of Christ. We saw in 1 Corinthians 12 that the metaphor of the body is one way the Scriptures help us consider ourselves and others in Christ. Reaching back to this image, we notice the importance of the little phrase in Acts 4:32 that the saints were of "one heart and mind." This little phrase explains the actions of the early church.

The Bible testifies that the body of Christ has one head, Christ Himself (see 1 Cor. 11:3; Eph. 4:15; 5:23; Col. 2:10). Since we have the same head, and He is the source and authority for the body, so our union with Him unifies our hearts and minds around the message of the gospel.

This is why the early church was quick to demonstrate their unity in their actions. Why wouldn't they be willing to share with those in need? Does the heart hoard all the blood? Do the lungs charge a fee for oxygen? Of course not! The body naturally helps and serves itself. This is what we see evidenced by our historical brothers and sisters and mothers and fathers in the faith.

> With what person would you say you are most united in mind and heart? How does that unity express itself? Where are there evidences of disunity?

> In what ways have you (or the church) potentially underestimated the power of personal generosity as a means to further the kingdom while on mission?

This common heart and mind is not only birthed out of the body metaphor, however. Because of their future hope, the early Christians were less likely to hold tightly to their present possessions.

Only the gospel can free men and women to be so generous because only the gospel calls such sacrifice a wise investment. This is what Jesus meant when He spoke about the necessity of present sacrifice for the sake of future glory. "Everyone who has left houses, brothers or sisters, father or mother, children, or fields because of My name will receive 100 times more and will inherit eternal life. But many who are first will be last, and the last first" (Matt. 19:29-30).

2 We Are Called to Be Holy

The church is to be of one heart and mind. We are also called to be holy—conformed not to this world but to our Father who has adopted us. The apostle Peter made this point when he based his call to holiness in God's holy character.

> [13] Therefore, with your minds ready for action, be serious and set your hope completely on the grace to be brought to you at the revelation of Jesus Christ. [14] As obedient children, do not be conformed to the desires of your former ignorance. [15] But as the One who called you is holy, you also are to be holy in all your conduct; [16] for it is written, Be holy, because I am holy.
>
> 1 PETER 1:13-16

Children love to imitate their heroes. Whether fictional or real, we have images of greatness that beckon to us. These are the elite and the sacred, and at least for a brief season in time, we seek to be like them. In the early 1990s, Gatorade came out with the "Be Like Mike" jingle. It instantly captured a part of the American spirit. Kids everywhere were striving toward a goal, but that goal was personified in one particular man. Those paying attention would see that not only were kids picking up on his talent but even his personality traits. Never before had so many children played a sport with their tongues hanging out of their mouths.

Greatness is like that. It whispers to us and compels us closer. God is like that. He is the very definition of sacred. He is set apart and distinct, entirely transcendent and yet wonderfully close. And He beckons us to be like Him. It is not enough to be good or do good; we are called to be like God Himself, the very definition of good.

Who did you seek to be like when you were a child? What did you do to pursue this?

Holiness and hope share more in common than just a few letters. According to Peter's first letter, it is the church's hope for the future that fuels the pursuit of holiness in the present. As Peter wrote, there is a "grace to be brought to you." The gospel is all grace, and we have experienced its abundance in the past and present. But the Scriptures here speak of a future grace.

What is this grace? Peter wrote that this grace will be ours "at the revelation of Jesus Christ." What does this mean? From the rest of the Scriptures, we can see that there is one particular promise that God has attached to the revealing of His Son—our resurrection— the day in which our bodies will be raised anew. No longer will be our bodies be afflicted by fatigue or flu, sickness or sin. We will be raised immortal, incorruptible, and imperishable (see 1 Cor. 15:51-57).

The glory of future grace isn't merely external though. As great and glorious as the idea of restored and resurrected bodies is, there is something else to consider as well. Just as these bodies will experience complete healing, so will our entire being experience deliverance from the tragic consequences of sin.

This means we will walk in holiness. Not partial holiness. We will not merely appear more holy. We will truly and completely experience total freedom from sin and all of its tragic effects. We will experience "wholeness," or *shalom* as our ancestors in the faith called it.

This helps us realize why Peter transitioned from the consideration of future glory to the present pursuit of holiness. Because we will experience full holiness in the future, our lives are to be marked by the passionate pursuit of holiness in the present. "Live like you will be" was his message. Since you will be fully holy then, passionately pursue holiness even now.

But how Peter made the argument is amazing. He didn't uphold holiness as some abstract virtue to pursue. It was not some theoretical standard of goodness or justice hanging over us for which we are to strive. Instead, he appealed to the nature and character of God Himself. In the age to come, we will be holy like God, so holiness is our profession now.

> What is the difference between seeing holiness as personal (about imitating God) and abstract (following a list of rules)?

> As one that has been sent by God, how does your pursuit of holiness empower you to fulfill God's mission in the world?

3 We Contend for the Faith of the Apostles

God has one church, one people who are called to be holy and to carry on the faith of the apostles. The letters of the New Testament exhort us to unity and holiness; they also encourage us to contend for the faith and deliver the gospel to the next generation. Take a look at Jude's instruction:

> Dear friends, although I was eager to write you about the salvation we share, I found it necessary to write and exhort you to contend for the faith that was delivered to the saints once for all.
> JUDE 3

Some things are worth defending, even at great cost. The gospel surely is. There is a faith worth contending for, a standard of teaching worth preaching and protecting and preserving, even at great personal cost. The gospel calls us to contend for this faith entrusted to us and to entrust it to others.

What few doctrines would you put in the very center of the faith—those you would deem essential for the protection of the apostolic deposit of doctrine?

What might be other doctrines that would lie outside that center?

Jude is one of the shortest books of the New Testament, but it is a powerfully profound book for the church today. From the theological richness of the opening benediction to the beautifully poetic closing doxology, there is an abundance of truth woven within its few words.

Jude's original desire was clear. He wanted to write an encouraging word. But something much more important prompted his pen to move in another direction. Certain false teachers had crept into the church and were seeking to upend it. Jude desired to write an exhortation but instead needed to warn those whom he loved against the false teachers. The church was "to contend for the faith that was delivered to the saints once for all."

The word *contend* contains the same root as agony. Various lexicons explain that the word is not passive but means, "to exert intense effort on behalf of something." [2]

As Christians, there are core beliefs that the church has always held as most precious and central. Historically, we have found the following to be in this category: the triune nature of God; the full deity and humanity of Christ; the truthfulness, sufficiency, and authority of Scripture; the substitutionary atoning death and resurrection of Jesus; justification by grace alone through faith alone; the bodily return of Christ; and the future resurrection and judgment.

> Which do you prefer—defending the Bible against skeptics or delivering the gospel to people who do not know Jesus? Why?

GROUP STUDY

Warm Up

When you stop and think about it, you are reading this material because of a long history. Peter, Paul, Stephen, Barnabas, and all the other apostles and their companions planted churches and trained pastors. Those churches then trained others to be sent out to plant other churches. One person told another person who told another the good news. For two thousand years, this has happened. Fathers and mothers have told daughters and sons. Men and women have told their neighbors. Others have traveled around the world to distant lands to share the good news.

Consider the very source for our "sentness." Read the following verses from the Book of John and discuss the missional mindset that has found its way in the Christian's spiritual DNA.

> [38] For I have come down from heaven not to do my will but to do the will of him who sent me. [39] And this is the will of him who sent me, that I shall lose none of all those he has given me, but raise them up at the last day.
> JOHN 6:38-39

> Jesus said to them, "If God were your Father, you would love me, for I have come here from God. I have not come on my own; God sent me.
> JOHN 8:42

> Again Jesus said, "Peace be with you! As the Father has sent me, I am sending you."
> JOHN 20:21

To what degree do you recognize your "sentness"—that you've already been sent by God?

List three or four values from Western culture that hinder the missional lifestyle. How do you overcome them?

Where are you going for God? Where is your church going for God?

Discussion

This is part of what it means to be the church. Not only do we have the opportunity and responsibility to contend for the gospel but also the call to deliver it to others. We have a responsibility to contend for the faith, and part of that contending includes a biblical call to entrust to others what has been entrusted to us (see 2 Tim. 2:1-2).

During this time you will have an opportunity to discuss what God revealed to you during the week. Listed below are some of the questions from your daily reading assignments. They will guide your small-group discussion.

1. Consider how strange the actions of the early believers must have been to outsiders. What reasons would you give to explain the early church's behavior?

2. In what ways have you (or the church) potentially underestimated the power of personal generosity as a means to further the kingdom while on mission?

3. What is the difference between seeing holiness as personal (about imitating God) and abstract (following a list of rules)?

4. As one that has been sent by God, how does your pursuit of holiness empower you to fulfill God's mission in the world?

5. What few doctrines would you put in the very center of the faith—those you would deem essential for the protection of the apostolic deposit of doctrine?

6. What might be other doctrines that would lie outside that center?

7. Which do you prefer—defending the Bible against skeptics or delivering the gospel to people who do not know Jesus? Why?

Conclusion

The church is united in heart and mind, holy as God is holy, and apostolic. But we are not only called to defend the truth but also sent to deliver it. This call to share the gospel with others includes not merely the fundamentals of the faith but indeed the full revelation of biblical truth.

In the Great Commission, Jesus told the disciples to teach others to observe "everything" He had commanded them (Matt. 28:18-20). As Paul addressed the Ephesian elders, he claimed his duty was to declare the "whole plan" or "whole counsel" of God (Acts 20:27). For both Jesus and Paul, the gospel is not to be broken down into important and unimportant parts. Everything that God says is important and is to be heeded.

Therefore, part of the call to contend for the faith includes not only a commission to preserve the universal boundaries of orthodoxy but to teach and preach the full counsel of God. This is especially important but also particularly difficult in a society that is growing less and less familiar with biblical truth and more and more comfortable with a culture of depravity.

Spend some time praying this for yourself and for your group:

"God, may You raise up churches that willingly contend for the faith!
Help us remain strong in You as we stand on Your truth. Unite us in
love as we share Christ to world. Give us new opportunities to bring
the message of Your Son to the next generation. Amen."

---

1. William Temple, quoted in *Creed*, by Winfield Bevins (Colorado Springs: NavPress, 2011), 63.
2. "ἐπαγωνίζομαι," *A Greek-English Lexicon of the New Testament and Other Early Christian Literature,* ed. Frederick William Danker, 3rd ed. (Chicago: University of Chicago Press, 2000), 356.
3. Dietrich Bonhoeffer, *Life Together* (New York: HarperOne, 1954), 30.

Christian brotherhood is not an ideal which we
must realize; it is rather a reality created by God
in Christ in which we may participate. [3]

DIETRICH BONHOEFFER

NOTES

Session 5

Dead to Ourselves

Christ says, "Give me All. I don't want so much of your time and so much of your money and so much of your work: I want You. I have not come to torment your natural self, but to kill it ...Hand over the whole natural self, all the desires which you think innocent as well as the ones you think wicked—the whole outfit. I will give you a new self instead. In fact, I will give you Myself: my own will shall become yours." [1]

C. S. LEWIS

INDIVIDUAL STUDY

Have you ever wished you could erase your identity and just start all over? In stressful moments, perhaps you've wanted to hit the reset button on life. Who doesn't have regrets? Who doesn't long for a fresh start in some areas? Sometimes it's because of the histories and circumstances of our past and present lives. Other times it's the residue of sin that clings to our hearts.

Our individual histories are cluttered with sin. For some it is a life of serious sexual sin; for others Pharisaical pride, greed, envy, laziness, apathy, complacency, and on and on we could go. Some lean toward "religious" sins while others are more prone to relativism. Our closets may be filled with skeletons of varying shapes and sizes, but all of us have them.

What is one circumstance in your past you wish you could change?

How has that circumstance affected your life?

When a computer's history is full with some secret sites and destructive documents, you can always hit erase, restore the computer, or just get a new one. But what about when our very hearts and minds are so filled with the virus of sin? The gospel provides an answer because the good news of Jesus Christ provides us with a new identity.

Who are we as God's people? One of the distinguishing marks of the church is that we are crucified with Christ. We are called to deny ourselves, die to certain desires, and suffer for doing good, according to God's will. As we are crucified to ourselves and our sinful desires, we showcase the glory of God to a watching world.

Throughout the week engage these daily study sections on your own. Each of these examines the different aspects of what it means to deny ourselves. There are three daily readings to prepare you before your group meets for this session. Interact with the Scriptures, and be ready to interact with your small group.

1 God's People Deny Themselves

Most of us are familiar with self-denial. Desiring to lose weight, we deny ourselves carbs or calories. Desiring to take that vacation we've always dreamed about, we cut our budget. Everyone practices some form of self-denial, and in this regard, Christians are no different. But the gospel calls us to a life of constant self-denial. We discipline ourselves for the sake of godliness. We're a people who seek lasting joy by denying ourselves passing pleasure. Jesus explained it this way:

> 24 Then Jesus said to His disciples, "If anyone wants to come with Me, he must deny himself, take up his cross, and follow Me. 25 For whoever wants to save his life will lose it, but whoever loses his life because of Me will find it. 26 What will it benefit a man if he gains the whole world yet loses his life? Or what will a man give in exchange for his life? 27 For the Son of Man is going to come with His angels in the glory of His Father, and then He will reward each according to what he has done. 28 I assure you: There are some standing here who will not taste death until they see the Son of Man coming in His kingdom."
>
> MATTHEW 16:24-28

All the apostles except John died a martyr's death. Peter, Andrew, Bartholomew, and Philip—crucified; Thomas—burned alive; Matthew and Paul—beheaded; and James—cast down from the temple and beaten. Persecution of Christians under the Emperors Nero and Diocletian was particularly gruesome. Believers were flayed, impaled, or covered in oil and set on fire. They were thrown to the lions, torn apart, and drowned at sea. But the church advanced as the kingdom of God took root in the hearts of people throughout the Roman Empire and beyond.

Though many of us may not face the torturous brutality inflicted upon our ancestors in the faith, we all face the same call from Christ to lay down our lives. Some will do so physically; all will do so spiritually. As we see in the words of Jesus, we are called to take up a cross and deny ourselves.

Do you think of self-denial as a good or bad? How could it be negative?

"Do what feels right"—this is the message of our culture, but not the message of our Lord. His was a much harder call. His was a charge that burrows into our hearts and minds and shatters our idyllic pursuit of utopian comfort and convenience. The call of Christ beckons us to deny ourselves. This isn't a message that is popular. It is not a message that tickles ears and pleases the lukewarm. It doesn't exactly appeal to the masses and crowds who just want to be happy. But it's the message of the King. The Christian life is a life of self-denial. It is a life of death.

We're called to so cherish and treasure the glory of Christ that the pleasures of this world pale in comparison. This isn't the message of one who was opposed to joy; this is the response of the One who knows where to find it. After all, what good is it to gain the world yet forfeit your soul?

What are some ways we can deny ourselves—at home, work, or church?

After calling His people to deny themselves, Christ gave another exhortation: Follow Me. Two simple words can have drastically different connotations depending on the context. For the person trailing the tour guide through the Old City of Jerusalem or the African savanna, the words carry a sense of adventure and awe. But what if the person speaking those words is heading up a hill? And what if that hill is where some of the grossest executions ever conceived were carried out? And what if that man is bloodied and beaten and carrying his own cross?

When Christ calls us to pick up our own cross, He is calling us to death. A person carrying their cross was a dead man walking. There would be no appeal or a last second stay of execution. To carry your cross was to die. That is the call of Christ.

For some the death that we are called to die for Christ is physical. Thousands upon thousands of our brothers and sisters around the world and throughout time have walked this road with Christ. Though such physical martyrdom seems far away from the contemporary comforts of our churches and couches, it is never too far away and could come soon to our doors.

As the gospel compels us to follow Christ, it charges us to die to our preferences and pleasures and to live to please God. It beckons us to mortify our pride and consider others more highly than ourselves. It demands that we lay down our rights and privileges and serve our neighbors. It exhorts us to crucify our resentment, bitterness, and hatred and instead to love our enemies and pray for them.

Think about the people closest to you. When we deny ourselves, how does this change the way we relate to them?

2 God's People Die to Certain Desires

The spiritual appetite is a bit like our own growing up. At some point, we've all enjoyed a variety of mushed carrots, peas, and bananas from little tiny jars. But we also drank our juicy-juice from sippy cups! Hopefully, we've all outgrown Gerber and moved on to the things that are a bit more substantive. What was once delightful is now distasteful. Conversely, the food we crave now never once crossed our minds as little babies. There are some things we are supposed to grow into. And subsequently, there are old desires from past appetites that no longer are appealing.

> **In what areas of your life have you experienced a change in appetite?**

In 1 Peter 4:1-2, we see how the suffering of Christ provides the fuel for our own response to tribulation and temptation. This truth builds upon what Peter had already written in 2:21 "For you were called to this, because Christ also suffered for you, leaving you an example, so that you should follow in His steps." Take a look:

> ¹ Therefore, since Christ suffered in the flesh, equip yourselves
> also with the same resolve—because the one who suffered in the
> flesh has finished with sin— ² in order to live the remaining time
> in the flesh, no longer for human desires, but for God's will.
> 1 PETER 4:1-2

As we follow Christ, we follow Him toward suffering. Some suffering is the result of external forces, such as persecution, sickness, etc. We will consider that aspect shortly. For now, we will focus on the internal conflict with residual sin.

Believers are called to follow Christ in radical commitment to cease following sin and instead to be ruled by the will of God. Because sin has been defeated and we have been released from its tyrannical rule, we are no longer to chase after it but instead to run hard after Christ.

This was the narrative of the great exodus event of the Old Testament. Seeing the Israelites freed from Egyptian slavery, modern readers of the text are shocked that Israel would long to return to it. Having witnessed God's power and experienced His provision, how could they grumble and groan and mumble and moan during their wilderness wanderings?

But are we really that different? Don't we all at times find ourselves like a dog returning to its vomit (Prov. 26:11) as we look back at the wasteland of our past and long for those passing pleasures? The call to crucify our passions and depraved desires is a call to stop drinking from tainted wells: "Be horrified at this, heavens; be shocked and utterly appalled. This is the Lord's declaration. For My people have committed a double evil: They have abandoned Me, the fountain of living water, and dug cisterns for themselves, cracked cisterns that cannot hold water" (Jer. 2:12-13).

Imagine living in a small cabin in the midst of majestic mountains. Having no access to electricity or utilities, you have to draw water each morning. Therefore, each day you wake up and head out on the porch in the cool, crisp morning. As you grab your bucket, you look to the right and see the most beautiful and crystal clear mountain stream you can imagine. You step off the porch, but instead of heading to the stream, you walk in the opposite direction. Having walked a short way, you stop at a hole that you dug months before. In the time since, the water has stagnated and filled with mud. It is infested with mosquito larvae and the droppings of animals having passed by. Undeterred, you plunge your bucket below the surface, and the rancid smell nearly overcomes you. Having drawn enough water for your morning rituals, you head back to the cabin and close the door behind you.

This is the image of our sin. Forsaking the fountain, we are foolishly content with filth.

When God calls for us to deny ourselves, He is calling for us to pursue a greater and more lasting joy. He is calling us to drink of better water. God is opposed to our incessant thirst for polluted waters that are unsatisfying and lethal. God is opposed to sin because sin is opposed to the ultimate joy and pleasure found only in His presence (Ps. 16:11).

What is your attitude toward your own sin? How can you tell when the Spirit is changing your mind and heart?

What are some human desires we should die to? What are some personal things that you need to see buried?

3 God's People Do Good as They Suffer

Suffering is often quite surprising—planes crash into skyscrapers, cancer strikes a loved one, the stock market plunges, and gunshots ring out in school hallways.

When Peter encouraged God's people not to be surprised with suffering, he was not commending stoicism or the ability to predict the future perfectly. He was not suggesting that we should have an "I knew it!" attitude when the tides and turmoil of life overtake us. What, then, was he saying? Look at his words in 1 Peter 4:12-19:

> 12 Dear friends, don't be surprised when the fiery ordeal comes among you to test you as if something unusual were happening to you. 13 Instead, rejoice as you share in the sufferings of the Messiah, so that you may also rejoice with great joy at the revelation of His glory. 14 If you are ridiculed for the name of Christ, you are blessed, because the Spirit of glory and of God rests on you. 15 None of you, however, should suffer as a murderer, a thief, an evildoer, or a meddler. 16 But if anyone suffers as a "Christian," he should not be ashamed but should glorify God in having that name. 17 For the time has come for judgment to begin with God's household, and if it begins with us, what will the outcome be for those who disobey the gospel of God? 18 And if a righteous person is saved with difficulty, what will become of the ungodly and the sinner? 19 So those who suffer according to God's will should, while doing what is good, entrust themselves to a faithful Creator.
>
> 1 PETER 4:12-19

In what ways have we Christians misunderstood the idea that God doesn't want us to suffer at all? How does the current culture support this idea?

In his letter, Peter was speaking specifically of persecution and the kind of suffering that comes from doing good in the presence of those who will not appreciate it (1 Pet. 2:19-20). He was writing of being "ridiculed for the name of Christ" and suffering specifically for being a Christian (4:14-16).

Though many of us in the Western church have not known the intensity of this type of suffering, we hear stories of our brothers and sisters across the world (1 Pet. 5:9). Even in the West, as the truths of Jesus Christ offend the sensibilities of the flesh, our culture is becoming increasingly more hostile to those who bear the name of "Christian."

This shouldn't surprise us. For Christ Himself told His followers the world would hate us the way the world hated Him (John 15:18-21). Christ's words are an important reminder that if we are being conformed into the image of a Suffering Servant, we should anticipate suffering as well. In fact, all those who want to live a godly life in Christ Jesus will be persecuted (2 Tim. 3:12).

God does not take pleasure in the suffering of His children, whom He loves. At the same time, there is a sense in which our suffering is according to His will. Consider the parents who allow their child to be exposed to chickenpox so that the disease will pass with relative risk compared to later danger. Do they want their child to be sick? In some sense they do, but only because they don't want a more serious sickness down the road. Think of the father who reprimands his son for running into the street without looking. He disciplines his son because he has a desire for the good and well-being of that son.

In what ways have you suffered for the name of Christ?

How do you discern between the sources of suffering—our flesh or sinful disobedience, the enemy's plan against us, the brokenness of this world, and for the sake of the gospel?

GROUP STUDY

Warm Up

Why does God allow His children to suffer? While we don't know every answer to that question, the Scriptures do give us at least a few answers—for our good, as a testimony for the world, and for His glory. They are listed below with a brief description. Take a moment to read them, and spend some time answering the question together.

How is suffering for our good? Part of that answer involves the role of suffering in relationship to God's discipline (Heb. 12:3-11). God disciplines us as a good Father who helps His children. His discipline is never without purpose. His discipline is designed to make us more like Him, to grant us greater sanctification.

How is our suffering a testimony to the world? "This man really was God's Son!" (Mark 15:39). This was the expression of the centurion overseeing Christ's crucifixion. Having witnessed the execution of an innocent man, the military commander's defenses were overcome. A similar phenomenon has occurred countless times throughout church history, from the accounts of the early church martyrs to the conversions of the tribe that murdered missionary Jim Elliot. In some strange but beautiful way, the suffering of saints is used by God to open the eyes and ears of others.

How does our suffering glorify God? God is glorified when men and women entrust themselves to Him. Finding Him faithful, we lay down our lives certain that He will raise them up again. Our suffering glorifies God when we say, "You are better." Our suffering glorifies God when we rest in His provision and protection and truly trust that the passing pain will be far surpassed by the eternal joy to come.

How has personal suffering ultimately led to your good?

In what ways has suffering brought glory to God?

How has your suffering forged a testimony that the world can see?

Discussion

Always be killing sin or it will be killing you. [2]

JOHN OWEN

We are a crucified people. In the death of Christ, we have died to our past in order to live for our King. We have been united in His suffering and death and given a new identity, a new hope, and a new purpose. During this time you will have an opportunity to discuss what God revealed to you during the week. Listed below are some of the questions from your daily reading assignments. They will guide your small-group discussion.

1. What is one circumstance in your past you wish you could change? How has that circumstance affected your life?

2. How do we as Christians deal with the tension of the seemingly paradoxical calls to enjoy good things and also deny ourselves?

3. Think about the people closest to you. When we deny ourselves, how does this change the way relate to them?

4. What is your attitude toward your own sin? How can you tell when the Spirit is changing your mind and heart?

5. What are some human desires we should die to? What are some personal things that you need to see buried?

6. In what ways have we Christians abandoned the idea that God doesn't want us to suffer at all? How does the current culture support this idea?

7. How do you discern between the sources of suffering—our flesh or sinful disobedience, the enemy's plan against us, the brokenness of this world, and for the sake of the gospel?

Conclusion

In light of the path that Jesus took, the path of obedience that accomplished for us our salvation, the question becomes, "Will we follow Him?" He suffered once for all necessarily; we now suffer willingly. This is what it means to follow Jesus and be a part of His church. You die to yourself by putting aside self-righteousness, self-indulgence, and everything that belongs to you—your desires, your ambitions, your thoughts, your dreams, and your possessions. At the same time, you take up your cross. For the early disciples, the language of taking up your cross would have immediately brought to mind images of crucifixion. Anyone carrying his cross was a dead man walking. Your life as you once knew it was over. [3]

DAVID PLATT

Spend some time praying this for yourself and for your group:

"God, show us daily what a life of self-denial looks like. Give us the grace to confess our sin. Lead us into a world that needs to see You, Jesus. Use our suffering for our good and Your glory! Amen."

1. C. S. Lewis, *Mere Christianity* (New York: Touchstone, 1996), 169.
2. John Owen, *The Mortification of Sin* (Carlisle, PA: Banner of Truth, 2004), 5.
3. David Platt, *Christ-Centered Exposition Commentary: Exalting Jesus in Matthew* (Nashville: B&H, 2013), 220.
4. Jim Elliot, quoted in *Good to Great in God's Eyes*, by Chip Ingram (Grand Rapids: Baker, 2007), 22.

He is no fool who gives what he cannot keep
to gain that which he cannot lose. [4]
JIM ELLIOT

NOTES

_____

_____

_____

_____

_____

_____

_____

_____

_____

_____

_____

_____

_____

_____

_____

THE GOSPEL PROJECT.

Session 6

Alive with Power

Knowing Christ means knowing the power of his resurrection and the fellowship of his suffering in the everyday events of our lives. The benefits of our future resurrection have been pulled back into the present with all its difficulties.

STEVE MATHEWSON

INDIVIDUAL STUDY

The accounts of Jesus' resurrection appearances to His disciples are gloriously odd. Take John's account of Jesus appearing to Mary Magdalene, for example. Here was a woman who knew Jesus well, a woman He delivered from demonic oppression. She saw Him crucified. She saw where He was buried. And yet, when He appeared to her, "she did not know it was Jesus" (John 20:14). Until He spoke her name, her eyes were not opened (20:16). And again in Luke we see a story of two disciples on the road to Emmaus. On their long journey, walking and talking with Jesus, they didn't recognize their Lord. Until He broke the bread, their eyes were not opened (see Luke 24:13-31).

Imagine knowing and loving someone for years and yet not immediately recognizing him or her. The oddness of these accounts is what we'd expect of first-century authors seeking to convey the truth of Jesus' resurrection body. It is the same body yet different in some ways.

As God's people, we too will one day be resurrected. We'll receive the "redemption of our bodies" (Rom. 8:23). But even though our bodily resurrection is reserved for the future, the New Testament teaches that those who have trusted Christ have already been raised to life. And like Jesus after His resurrection, we are the same and yet different in important ways. There is a discontinuity between our past and present. Those who have been rescued from slavery to sin and death and raised to new life are no longer immediately recognizable to the world.

> **When has someone told you before, "You've changed," or, "You're different now"? What were they referring to?**

> **What are some pieces of evidence that would indicate a person has been spiritually transformed?**

In this session, we'll look at the implications of the resurrection for the Christian life. We're not only crucified with Christ but also raised with Him to walk in a new way of life. Through the power of the Spirit, God the Father has rescued us from the tyranny of sin and death and made us alive with Christ. Freed from sin's rule, we now live for righteousness.

Throughout the week engage these daily study sections on your own. Each of these examines the different aspects of our power that comes from God. There are three daily readings to prepare you before your group meets for this session. Interact with the Scriptures, and be ready to interact with your small group.

1 Made Alive with Christ

Zombies are everywhere these days—from major motion pictures to YouTube videos and hit television shows. Even scientific journals and news programs are getting in on the action. It seems the Western world is obsessed with the undead. In most depictions, zombies are physically slow and deteriorating. They are isolated and show no signs of social interaction or love. They are driven by hunger. They know no pain or joy; they only crave. Some of these same signs are present in humanity when we are dominated by "the flesh"—our sinful nature.

When the Bible describes those who have been raised from the dead, we see an altogether different picture. In fact, in just about every way, we are the exact opposite of zombies. Having died to sin, we are enabled to experience a greater and greater capacity to feel and love and serve. We are able to deny our cravings and to run toward a greater joy. Far from being isolated and individualistic, our hearts and minds are united such that we enter into the pain and sorrow of those who walk alongside us.

Having been crucified with Christ, we have died to sin and our old way of life and are freed to walk toward the new life He provides. In Romans, Paul wrote about baptism as a signpost for the death and resurrection of Christ. In baptism, we have symbolically entered into the death and resurrection of our Lord. This makes all the difference in the world in our relationship to sin.

> [1] What should we say then? Should we continue in sin so that grace may multiply? [2] Absolutely not! How can we who died to sin still live in it? [3] Or are you unaware that all of us who were baptized into Christ Jesus were baptized into His death? [4] Therefore we were buried with Him by baptism into death, in order that, just as Christ was raised from the dead by the glory of the Father, so we too may walk in a new way of life.
> ROMANS 6:1-4

Think about the last time you saw a baptism. What elements of baptism represent death and resurrection?

Romans 6 begins by answering a question raised by the last part of the previous chapter: "The law came along to multiply the trespass. But where sin multiplied, grace multiplied even more so that, just as sin reigned in death, so also grace will reign through righteousness, resulting in eternal life through Jesus Christ our Lord" (Rom. 5:20-21). The more sin that God forgives, the more grace He displays. The more grace He displays, the more glory He receives. If grace lifts us out of the abyss of sin, then wouldn't a deeper hole merely serve to manifest more grace?

It sounds right. If God is glorified by displaying grace, then why shouldn't we sin more? That's the context of the opening verses of Romans 6. Paul's response was quick and emphatic— "Absolutely not!" It's a strong denial of this false inference and misapplication of God's grace.

Paul's argument for the falsehood of such an idea is based in the reality that theologians have called "union with Christ." We should not and indeed cannot continue to live in sin because we have been united with Christ not only in His death (which we have discussed previously) but also in His resurrected life. This doctrine of union with Christ saturates the New Testament Scriptures. Here are just a few of the passages:

> [1] Therefore, no condemnation now exists for those in Christ Jesus, [2] because the
> Spirit's law of life in Christ Jesus has set you free from the law of sin and of death.
> **ROMANS 8:1-2**

> [30] But it is from Him that you are in Christ Jesus, who became God-given
> wisdom for us—our righteousness, sanctification, and redemption, [31] in
> order that, as it is written: The one who boasts must boast in the Lord.
> **1 CORINTHIANS 1:30-31**

> Therefore, if anyone is in Christ, he is a new creation; old things
> have passed away, and look, new things have come.
> **2 CORINTHIANS 5:17**

Having died to sin, it no longer is our master. Its dominion was broken and we were set free. How then shall we live? Paul wrote we are freed to "walk in a new way of life" (Rom. 6:4). This profound statement touches every aspect of our lives. Life is lived in a new way. Having died to the love of self, we're made alive to love and serve God and others. The gospel affects everything.

What does it mean to have "died to sin" if we still sin?

**The union we have with Christ gives us the freedom to walk a new life.
How have you stepped into that new life? What does it look like on the
inside and out?**

2 Made Alive to God

We are not simply made alive with Christ; we are also made alive to God. Our direction, our outlook, and our orientation are turned away from self and sin and toward God and righteousness. Watch how Paul continued his teaching on our union with Christ:

> [5] For if we have been joined with Him in the likeness of His death, we will certainly also be in the likeness of His resurrection. [6] For we know that our old self was crucified with Him in order that sin's dominion over the body may be abolished, so that we may no longer be enslaved to sin, [7] since a person who has died is freed from sin's claims. [8] Now if we died with Christ, we believe that we will also live with Him, [9] because we know that Christ, having been raised from the dead, will not die again. Death no longer rules over Him. [10] For in light of the fact that He died, He died to sin once for all; but in light of the fact that He lives, He lives to God. [11] So, you too consider yourselves dead to sin but alive to God in Christ Jesus.
>
> ROMANS 6:5-11

The story of the exodus and Israel's liberation from Egypt is a physical representation of the spiritual reality that has been accomplished in Christ. Our release from the mastery of sin is likened to the redemption of Israel. In the words of the gospel, we are liberated from our iniquity, as death itself lies dying.

United with Christ in His death, we also share in His resurrection. That power has been released even now in the new life we are given as believers. It will be manifested even more when broken and beaten bodies are raised from the dust incorruptible, immortal, and imperishable.

What do you think it means to "live to God"? What demands does this make upon our lives?

Being made "alive to God" is not temporary or reversible. As Christ shall never again die, neither shall we. Sin and death have lost their hold on us (Rom. 6:6-7). We are free!

"Free at last!" These were the words of the old spiritual quoted by Martin Luther King Jr. in his famous "I Have a Dream" speech. These are fitting words for countless African Americans dispossessed by the residue of hundreds of years of racial bigotry, intolerance, and sweltering injustice.

These are fitting words for the Christian experience as well. In essence, all sin is enslaving. As Jesus said, "Everyone who commits sin is a slave of sin" (John 8:34). But if we have died, then we are no longer under its inflexible and absolute rule. Instead, we have been set free. As Israel in the wilderness no longer had a quota of bricks to produce, so we are free from obligation to the flesh.

Since we are set free from sin, we are not liberated to sin again. Does Christ ever heal and then say, "Go and sin some more"? Of course not! When we die to sin, we are made alive to something, actually some One. In our death to sin, we experience life to God. The resurrected life means we are set free from the slavery of selfishness and redeemed to walk in obedience to Christ.

Having been set free and given life, we now find the first command in the entire Book of Romans. After this chapter, Paul doesn't return again to commands for another six chapters, so this first appearance of a command is quite significant. Look at verse 11 again: "So, you too consider yourselves dead to sin but alive to God in Christ Jesus."

In what areas of your life do you feel as though you are still living in chains and darkness?

How might the message of the gospel proclaim and provide freedom in those areas?

3 Made Alive for Righteousness

¹² Therefore do not let sin reign in your mortal body, so that you obey its desires.
¹³ And do not offer any parts of it to sin as weapons for unrighteousness.
But as those who are alive from the dead, offer yourselves to God, and
all the parts of yourselves to God as weapons for righteousness. ¹⁴ For sin
will not rule over you, because you are not under law but under grace.

ROMANS 6:12-14

In verse 13, we are told we could use our bodies as weapons for unrighteousness or for righteousness. Just about anything can be a weapon. The Jason Bourne films showed a man who could fight armed assassins with a hardcover book, a rolled up magazine, a towel, a fountain pen, and an electrical cord. He also used an oscillating fan, a flashlight, and aerosol as diversions to help him escape. He is a cross between MacGyver and Kevin McCallister from *Home Alone*.

What does it mean to think of ourselves as weapons for righteousness?
How can our hands and feet be weapons for righteousness?

Because of Christ's resurrection, sin has been displaced in our lives. It has been robbed of power and prestige and replaced by another who is more powerful. Why, then, would we give it our homage and obedience? This is Paul's point. Having its tyranny overthrown, why would we again submit to its slavery?

As Paul spoke of our call to pursue sanctification as a resurrected people, he used violent images to express the seriousness of our task. Elsewhere he wrote that we are to mortify the flesh. We kill sin. We wage war against sin. This is not the time or task for casualness and comfort; this is a time for violence and warfare. And all of our effort and energy are turned toward this pursuit of righteousness now that we have been set free and made alive in Christ.

He continued: "Do not offer any parts of [your body] to sin as weapons for unrighteousness" (v. 13). There are countless ways that we can fail to follow this command. Our hearts are quick to drift, and our hands and feet soon follow. We are a people "prone to wander" as the hymn declares.

A little later, Paul wrote the following that complements well what we have just considered:

> I am using a human analogy because of the weakness of your flesh.
> For just as you offered the parts of yourselves as slaves to moral
> impurity, and to greater and greater lawlessness, so now offer them
> as slaves to righteousness, which results in sanctification.
> ROMANS 6:19

As our members once served as our enemies, now they are to be stewarded as allies. With the same intensity that we once pursued sin, so we are now freed to pursue righteousness. Having died to sin, we are set free from its dominion. Therefore, we are not to return to the land of our slavery. Instead, we are to walk in the light of our liberty by pursuing righteousness.

The very last word of verse 14 fills us in on what empowers our obedience: grace. Grace is what the gospel is all about. From beginning to end, from liberty to life, the gospel is the good news of God's grace.

Grace is what provides the power for our obedience, but we can be even more specific. The particular grace that is given to us is the grace of God's personal presence—the Holy Spirit. As Romans 8 says, it is "by the Spirit" that we are to put sin to death and walk in life: "So then, brothers, we are not obligated to the flesh to live according to the flesh, for if you live according to the flesh, you are going to die. But if by the Spirit you put to death the deeds of the body, you will live" (Rom. 8:12-13).

Move from theory to practice. What does pursuing righteousness look like Sunday through Saturday?

What role does your community of faith play as you put the deeds of the body to death?

GROUP STUDY

Warm Up

We need to be reminded from time to time how much power we have in Christ. When God brought us back to life, He didn't give us a wimpy life—He gave us the victorious life filled with power!

Read these passages of Scripture. Each one focuses on the things of God that are alive and powerful and have been given to us—His Spirit, word, life, love, and identity!

> 10 But if Christ is in you, then even though your body is subject to death because of sin, the Spirit gives life because of righteousness. 11 And if the Spirit of him who raised Jesus from the dead is living in you, he who raised Christ from the dead will also give life to your mortal bodies because of his Spirit who lives in you.
> ROMANS 8:10-11

> For the word of God is alive and active. Sharper than any double-edged sword, it penetrates even to dividing soul and spirit, joints and marrow; it judges the thoughts and attitudes of the heart.
> HEBREWS 4:12

> 37 No, in all these things we are more than conquerors through him who loved us. 38 For I am convinced that neither death nor life, neither angels nor demons, neither the present nor the future, nor any powers, 39 neither height nor depth, nor anything else in all creation, will be able to separate us from the love of God that is in Christ Jesus our Lord.
> ROMANS 8:37-39

Who needs to be encouraged right now? Spend some time in prayer for those who are discouraged.

Discussion

Since Christ's death led to his resurrection and a new
life, so in the same way our union with Christ will, and
must, lead to a new life ... If we believe in Christ, a change
of life will happen. We will not live in sin anymore.[2]

TIM KELLER

During this time you will have an opportunity to discuss what God revealed to you during the week. Listed below are some of the questions from your daily reading assignments. They will guide your small-group discussion.

1. What does it mean to have "died to sin" if we still sin?

2. The union we have with Christ gives us the freedom to walk a new life. How have you stepped into that new life? What does it look like on the inside and out?

3. What do you think it means to "live to God"? What demands does this make upon our lives?

4. In what areas of your life do you feel as though you are still living in chains and darkness? How might the message of the gospel proclaim and provide freedom in those areas?

5. What does it mean to think of ourselves as weapons for righteousness? How can our hands and feet be weapons for righteousness?

6. Move from theory to practice. What does pursuing righteousness look like Sunday through Saturday?

7. What role does your community of faith play as you put the deeds of the body to death?

Conclusion

When the Lord redeemed Israel, He did not merely say, "You are free. Go ahead now, and I'll meet you in Canaan." What an affliction that would have been! Israel would have made it no farther than the edge of the Red Sea before being swallowed by Pharaoh's army. Even those who possibly escaped would have perished of hunger and thirst in the wilderness.

God did not merely set an appointment to meet up in the promised land. He personally dwelt among His people and went before and behind them, providing for them manna and water and instruction along the way.

Likewise, Christ does not merely set us free from sin and say, "Go and sin no more." Instead, He is with us always by the power and presence of the Holy Spirit. This is grace—God within us, providing for us, preserving us, protecting us, instructing us, empowering us on mission. This is the grace that we are now under in the gospel. This is good news indeed.

Spend some time praying this for yourself and for your group:

"God, through Your Son, teach us what self-denial looks like. Help us to encourage one another as we choose to die to ourselves and live for You. Give us a desire to pursue the righteousness that comes from knowing Jesus. Amen."

1. Steve Mathewson, in "The Resurrection Changes Everything: A Conversation with Steve Mathewson," by Trevin Wax, Kingdom People [online], 24 January 2013 [cited 26 June 2014]. Available from the Internet: *thegospelcoalition.org.*
2. Timothy Keller, *Romans 1–7 for You* (The Good Book Company, 2014), 140.
3. Cyril of Alexandria, *Explanation of the Letter to the Romans,* quoted in *Romans,* ed. Gerald Bray, vol. VI in *Ancient Christian Commentary: New Testament* (Downers Grove: IVP, 1998), 156.

As we have been buried, so we must rise with Christ in a spiritual sense. For if to be buried together with Christ means dying to sin, then it is clear that rising with him means living in righteousness.[3]

CYRIL OF ALEXANDRIA

NOTES

SMALL-GROUP TIPS

Reading through this section and utilizing the suggested principles and practices will greatly enhance the group experience. First is to accept your limitations. You cannot transform a life. Your group must be devoted to the Bible, the Holy Spirit, and the power of Christian community. In doing so your group will have all the tools necessary to draw closer to God and to each other—and to experience heart transformation.

GENERAL TIPS:

- Prepare for each meeting by reviewing the material, praying for each group member, and asking the Holy Spirit to work through you as you point to Jesus each week.

- Make new attendees feel welcome.

- Think of ways to connect with group members away from group time. The amount of participation you have during your group meetings is directly related to the amount of time you connect with your group members away from the group meeting. Consider sending e-mails, texts, or social networking messages encouraging members in their personal devotion times prior to the session.

MATERIALS NEEDED:

- Bible

- Bible study book

- Pen/pencil

PROVIDE RESOURCES FOR GUESTS:

- An inexpensive way to make first-time guests feel welcome is to provide them a copy of your Bible study book. Estimate how many first-time guests you can expect during the course of your study, and secure that number of books. What about people who have not yet visited your group? You can encourage them to visit by providing a copy of the Bible study book.

SMALL-GROUP VALUES

Meeting together to study God's Word and experience life together is an exciting adventure. Here are values to consider for small-group experiences:

COMMUNITY: God is relational, so He created us to live in relationship with Him and one another. Authentic community involves sharing life together and connecting on many levels with others in our group.

INTERACTIVE BIBLE STUDY: God gave us the Bible—His great story of redeeming people from sin and death. We need to deepen our understanding of God's Word. People learn and remember more as they wrestle with truth and learn from others. Bible discovery and group interaction will enhance spiritual growth.

EXPERIENTIAL GROWTH: Beyond solely reading, studying, and dissecting the Bible, being a disciple of Christ involves marrying knowledge and experience. We do this by taking questions to God, opening a dialogue with our hearts, and utilizing other ways to listen to God speak (other people, nature, circumstances, etc.). Experiential growth is always grounded in the Bible as God's primary revelation and our ultimate truth-source.

POWER OF GOD: Processes and strategies will be ineffective unless we invite and embrace the presence and power of God. In order to experience community and growth, Jesus needs to be the centerpiece of our group experiences, and the Holy Spirit must be at work.

REDEMPTIVE COMMUNITY: Healing best occurs within the context of community and relationships. It's vital to see ourselves through the eyes of others, share our stories, and ultimately find freedom from the secrets and lies that enslave our souls.

MISSION: God has invited us into a larger story with a great mission of setting captives free and healing the broken-hearted (see Isa. 61:1-2). However, we can only join in this mission to the degree that we've let Jesus bind up our wounds and set us free. Others will be attracted to an authentic, redemptive community.

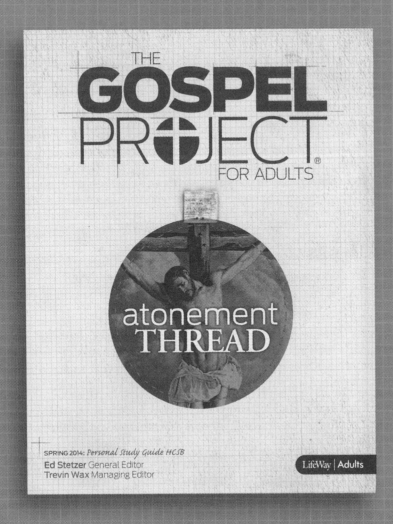